Personal
Effectiveness

Personal
Effectiveness

How to Profit from your Potentials

Sylvester Okoyomon

Personal Effectiveness

How to Profit from Your Potentials

Copyright © 2017 by Sylvester Okoyomon

All Rights Reserved. No part of this book may be reproduced, stored in a retrievable system, transmitted in any form, or by any means, electronic, mechanical, photocopying, recording, or otherwise, without prior written permission from the author.

Dedication

To the busy corporate executive, to the stay at home mum; to the startup entrepreneur, the college student; to the artist, the stylist; to everyone who feels like there's more to this life than just living and dying.

Contents

Introduction *1*

1. Potential 6

2. Process 13

3. Platform 25

4. Profit 38

Closing *41*

Introduction

Do you know any really gifted individual? You feel like there's something special about this fellow. When you are with him, just listening to him talk, you feel like screaming to the whole world to watch out for this rising star. You heard her sing like an angel and you were so sure that Celine Dion and Mariah Carey had gotten their job cut out for them. He was very energetic and athletic, easily an Olympic medal material, but several years later, these same people seem stuck in one spot. They are unknown, uncelebrated and broke despite being very gifted. Do you know anyone who seems to be all potential but no profit? Or maybe the description fits you. Do you feel like you have so much potential but fear you are not making much of what you've got? Believe me, I know how it feels because that was my story until I decided to take some steps. In this book, I document the things I have learnt so far on this journey. There are many talented and gifted persons wasting away because they do not know how to profit with their

Personal Effectiveness

gifts and talents.

There's an interesting narrative about three servants whose master went on a long trip. Before he set out, he gave them large sums of money and asked each person to 'do business' with the money received. He did not, however, give them the same amounts of money. To one he gave five talents, the other two talents, and the third guy was given one talent.

As the story goes, after a long while the master returned from his trip and asked to see their account balances. The guy with five talents traded with his talents and got five more talents (he made more money); same thing for the fellow with two talents. He made two more talents. Their master was impressed with their profits. He praised them. But the fellow with one talent did not trade with his own talent. He rather hid it by digging a hole in the ground and buried his master's money. With him, the master was furious and said "Are you kidding me! Couldn't you at least invest in M.M.M[1]?"

Oops! Scratch that.

It was just my imagination. The master said no such thing. Anyway, according to the story, the master accused this servant of being a criminal for living so cautiously. He pointed out that the money could have been kept in the bank to at least yield some interest. By the way, did I remember to tell you that this story is found in the bible? I guess I also forgot to tell you that the word 'talent' used in most bible versions was actually a measurement of money in those days meaning a 'talent weight of gold'. You see,

Introduction

back then your money was measured by how it compares in value to weights of gold. Experts say a talent spoken of in those days is estimated to be between $1,000 and $30,000 in today's currency. Now if you convert that to the currency in your country you begin to get the picture of what these three guys were handling. This is serious stuff here. In my country, for instance, these guys would be millionaires!

Here's why I brought up this story. Our lives on earth can be compared to those servants who were given talents of money to profit with. "But Sylvester, no one has given me any money to keep or trade with," you say. Ah! Then you miss the point. What you and I have been given are not talents of money, but talents of treasures in the form of potentials and abilities. You and I have been given deposits of natural abilities deep inside our unique personalities. Wouldn't you want to be like those two servants who made profits with their resources rather than the other lazy servant?

My goal in writing this book is to help you become aware that you are a treasure chest of gifts and abilities. Not only that, I'll show you how to locate these treasures and develop them for profitable use. I call it being personally effective.

What then is Personal Effectiveness? It is simply profiting from your potentials. Personal Effectiveness in this context is the maximum utilization of all the abilities that you have. It is being all you were meant to be by living out your full potentials. It is having a life of influence and affluence through the proper use of your inward and outward resources. It is being fulfilled by knowing that your life has a purpose and doing all you can to live out that purpose. One dear gentleman calls it living intentionally. I call it living effectively. Dear friend, life's original intent is for you to profit from your potentials.

Let's assume you use the engine of a fighter jet to power your lawnmower. The fact that it worked doesn't mean that you have put that engine to effective use; we would say that the engine is not being used to its full potential. In the same manner, many people do not live up to their full potentials. They miss out on all the profits they could have accrued by being all they could be. In the words of Phillips Brooks, "When you discover you have been leading only half a life, the other half is going to haunt you until you develop it".

Come; let's go on this journey to fame and fortune through the proper discovery, development, and deployment of our personal resources. Let me be your

Introduction

guide to mastering the business of your talents. The journey begins here.

Your Life Coach,

Sylvester Okoyomon

Chapter One

Potential

The word 'potential' refers to the latent qualities and abilities that an individual possesses which may be developed for future success or usefulness. These abilities are basically natural.

In life, we are all naturally good at something. Whether it is an ability to sing, dance, act, write, compose, persuade, repair, organize or design. We are not all gifted with the same things. For instance, some people are naturally good with numbers. They have numerate abilities; some others are gifted with humor - the ability to see the funny side of things. The list of possible talents is endless. However, I am sure you get the point. We all have unique natural abilities.

Potential

In the pursuit of success, happiness and personal effectiveness, the journey often begins with *under-standing* your abilities, gifts or talents. Martin Seligman, in his book *Authentic Happiness,* said: "The good life consists in deriving happiness by using your signature strengths every day in the main realms of living".

It means that anyone and everyone can be successful because everyone has at least one talent or signature strength. Everyone has at least one thing they are good at. In case you've ever felt like a loser or a failure, this is good news. Maybe people have called you a 'never do well' or you've had so many failures, you wonder if you could ever get anything right in your life; well, I've got good news for you. The good news is that all you need to be successful and effective already lies in you. It is called your potential . . . your natural ability . . . your gift or talent. Your primary assignment is to discover it. Find out the one thing that you can do better than most people.

 You Are a Treasure Chest

Did you notice that our opening definition of potential mentioned something about 'latent'? The word latent is a synonym or old English expression for 'hidden' or 'dormant'. Your potential refers to those gifts hidden inside you which may not necessarily manifest readily. They are hidden just like treasures are hidden in a chest; therefore, it takes a careful search to discover them.

Look at it this way; the most precious things are usually hidden from plain sight. Where do you find, silver, gold, or diamond? I bet you can't find them in their raw form just along the road as you take a casual stroll. To get diamonds, you must dig deep beneath the earth. Bottom line: treasures are often meant to be 'dug out'.

You are a sort of treasure chest—a box of treasures if you will. Hidden deep within you are special gifts, talents and abilities. For most people, these abilities or potentials remain undiscovered and untapped which explains why they lead unfulfilled and unproductive lives.

Lessons from the Field of Exploration

To explore, means to examine or evaluate. It also means 'to search for mineral resources'. Wikipedia defines it as the *act of searching for the purpose of discovery of information or resources.*

Take Oil and Gas exploration as an example. The goal is to seek for Hydrocarbon deposits located deep beneath the earth surface using seismic survey technologies.

Geologists look for what they call a 'prospect'—a potential trap which they believe may contain *hydrocarbons*. Once their suspicion is confirmed, they 'harvest' the crude for onward refinement.

Potential

Just as the discovery of these natural resources embedded deep under the earth make for riches and profit for their host countries or communities, do you know that you have embedded resources in you which if you were to discover and tap them would bring you riches and influence? Learn from the oil prospecting companies. Dig deep. Locate your own gold, or oil. We call them POTENTIALS.

Like the slogan used in the Peak milk advert many years ago, "It's in you". Success is in you, it lies in your potentials, but you have some EXPLORATION to do. You must go into the deep recess of your personality and search out those hidden treasures called your gifts and talents. You may need to sit with a coach to help you in one or two 'discovery sessions'. Remember, you are a living, breathing and walking treasure chest. Find your treasure!

Undertake an intensive personal analysis. Take a piece of paper, write down all the things you can do very well. Recall any project, test or assignment you did very well in the past. What activities have you excelled in? It is important you identify your potentials because they are your seeds for greatness. There's another bible story of a widow who needed help and ran to a prophet. The prophet asked her a simple question: "What do you have in your house?"

Therefore, I ask you too: What do you have in your house? Or, let me rephrase that: What do you have in you? What do you have to offer your world?

Personal Effectiveness

 ## "Who Potential Epp?"[2]

Lisa Nichols, bestselling author, and CEO of Motivating the Masses was so broke at a time in her life that she could not afford to buy diapers for her 8 - month old baby. She had to wrap him in a towel for a couple of days. But something happened in her mind at that period. She made up her mind never to be broke again. Today, now worth millions of dollars and the head of one of the top training and development companies in the world, Lisa recalls in an interview with Steve Harvey that even while she was broke back then, she was aware she had potentials inside of her. And in her words, "I was tired of having potential".

You see my friends, recognizing that you have potential is only the first step. Like Lisa, you may be aware of your potentials. This is good. But it does not end there. In my country Nigeria, we would say "Who potential epp?" Talent is not enough; Okay, for emphasis, let me say it like this: TALENT IS OVERRATED! The streets are littered with talented people. You need to do something with your talent or else you will still end up broke, unrecognized and unrewarded.

 ## Potential Must Be Developed

By definition, it appears there is an uncertainty or

probability about potential. Its usefulness depends on 'if it is developed'. Friends, there's something 'iffy' about life. You are never guaranteed of any outcome. It always depends on what you are willing and ready to do.

A potential is only a capacity. It's like startup capital. Look at it this way, you may have the capacity to be a great lawyer but never become one. A boy has the potential to become a man, but (for some reason or several reasons) may not develop into a man.

It is sad to note that there are many potential millionaires, potential superstars, potential champion-ship athletes, potential technological gurus, potential celebrity caterers and fashion icons. But many of them die with their potentials in the raw, untapped and undeveloped form. They die without the influence and fortune that could have been theirs. They die without becoming personally effective. The reason is found in the next chapter.

However, here are a few things you can do to apply what you've learned so far.

Critical Action Steps

1) *Undergo a personal SWOT analysis. SWOT is an acronym for* **Strengths, Weaknesses, Opportunities,** *and* **Threats.** *Take personality tests. There are several free tests online. Discover your uniqueness. Know yourself.*

Personal Effectiveness

2) *Seek feedback from trusted friends and family members. Find out where you have the greatest return on investment. In other words, what are those areas in your life where a seemingly little effort produces large results? What do people say you are good at?*

Chapter Two

Process

The Oxford Dictionary defines the word 'process' as *'a series of things that are done in order to achieve a particular result'*.

Another definition says, *'a series of things that happen naturally and result in gradual change'*.

Now you've identified your potentials. What next? Start processing. Your potentials need to be processed. Just about all of life involves a process. Growing up from a baby to an adult is a process; cooking your favorite meal involves a process. Between the planting and harvesting of crops, there is a process. In the same way, your journey to personal effectiveness and success involves a process . . . the processing of your potentials, that is.

All Processing Takes Time

'Please wait while your transaction is processing'. You hear that statement every time you visit the ATM stand. In a melodious, recorded voice prompt, we are daily reminded as we queue to collect our much-needed cash that all processing takes time, hence the need to wait. And when the voice tells you to wait, you do just that. Don't you?

I am often amused when I hear young people say things like "I wan blow" (A Nigerian vernacular loosely translated as "I want to become successful, rich or famous"). Usually, these young, vibrant dreamers are ignorant of the process involved in the pursuit of their desired success. For many of them, they dream of overnight success, overnight fame, or overnight fortune. Life doesn't work that way—ask any farmer.

You see, farmers are very sensible individuals. When they plant seeds, they know that it takes time to harvest so they do not bother digging up their seeds every day. They patiently wait. You too must learn to wait. The effective life will not happen overnight. In the words of Epictetus, the Greek Philosopher, "No great thing is created suddenly". My goal is to help you achieve personal success—realistically.

Again, from our definitions of the word Process, notice two striking clauses:

Process

'A series of things are done' and 'a series of things happen naturally'. In every process, one or both of these clauses come into play. A practical example is planting. During planting season, a farmer carries out several activities. He clears the field (farm), digs the earth and plants the seed. These are all things the farmer must do if he wants a harvest.

 Training

Your talent or gift like a seed must be planted. Your 'planting activities' will include all those things necessary to develop your potentials into something more valuable namely, SKILLS.

You see, my dear friend, people don't pay for potentials. They pay for the skills which solve problems. While they may admire your potentials, they are more likely to put their money on your skills instead. Remember I said earlier that your potential is only a probability. Like a seed, it may or may not germinate and 'investors' don't like uncertainty. For those of you who have often wondered while banks usually don't give loans to startups and 'up-coming' entrepreneurs, there you have it.

Your dream, your idea—that thing you say you want to be and do, is still in its potential form, it goes with a lot of uncertainty. No one wants to bet on you yet until you prove your worth. This is why you must turn your potentials to

Personal Effectiveness

skills by training.

Training is a key element of the process to personal effectiveness and success. You have to go on personal development training. No training session or season is easy; ask any athlete or professional footballer. It involves a lot of discipline and focus. Engage in personal and professional training. Refine those abilities in you as you develop skill.

Your training will involve LEARNING; reading the right books, acquiring education and information, formally and/or informally in your area of gifting. I can almost hear you say, "If I'm gifted in an area, why do I need to study it again?" The answer is simple. There is a difference between raw food and cooked food; crude oil and refined petroleum products. Your natural abilities are largely raw talents. Learning is a refining process. It polishes your potential. It is a vital part of the process.

Your training will also involve PRACTICE. Have you ever heard about the 10,000-Hour Rule? Made popular by the author Malcolm Gladwell, the principle holds that 10,000 hours of "deliberate practice" are needed to become world class in any field.

Another vital aspect of the process of developing your talents into skills is mentorship. You need a mentor (or even mentors). A mentor is someone who can guide you and hopefully reduce the possibility of needless mistakes. Your mentor is someone who has been where you are aspiring to get to. He has 'been there, done that' as we say.

Make no mistake, you need to learn the ropes and be taught by someone or some people—whether directly or indirectly. You need someone to call for validation and support when you are about to take some critical steps on your journey to personal effectiveness and success. You need a guide by your side at those critical moments when you are scared and unsure of yourself.

Many people want to succeed but do not want to go through the process. No wonder they die with their potentials. Let this not be your story.

Let's get back to our analogy of the farmer . . .

He clears the grass, digs the soil and plants his seed. He periodically waters and weeds as the need arise. However, there is a part of the process he has no control over and that is, the actual germination or growth of the crop. That happens on its own—naturally. Only nature controls that.

 Failure

You may be wondering why I mention 'failure' in a book that speaks about success? Remember how we said that part of the process includes 'a series of things that happen naturally'? Failure is part of that series of things that happen naturally. You may have to go through a series of failures in your attempt to be successful. It was Sir Thomas J. Watson, the American businessman and CEO of International Business Machines (IBM) who once said "If you want to increase your success rate, double your failure rate"; success is on the other side of failure.

So you see my dear friend, contrary to what we were taught in school, failure is your school teacher. The inventor, Thomas Edison failed very many times in his light bulb experiment until he got it right. When asked, he acknowledged that all those failed experiments were not failures in themselves, but that he was learning the process, knowing what works and what doesn't. That's a good attitude. Have you failed at anything? Does it seem like your best attempts to build a business or advance your career seem to hit the rocks? Cheer up friend, you are in good company. It's part of the process.

A key attitude to imbibe in your training process will be humility and patience. You will go through times when it does not seem like you will ever be all you dreamed of becoming. Those are periods requiring patience.

Lessons from the Butterfly

The female butterfly lays her eggs on leaves and waits for them to hatch. Just as the hen's eggs hatch into chickens, the butterfly's' eggs should hatch into little butterflies, right? Well, not exactly.

In the case of the butterfly, there is a 4-stage life cycle.

Process

In stage one, you have the eggs. In stage two each egg hatches into a larva called a Caterpillar. Ever seen one of those Caterpillars? They are like huge maggots ...very ugly and unappealing worms! However, something wonderful happens in the final stage (Stage 4)—a beautiful butterfly emerges.

Just as the seemingly "ugly' Caterpillar undergoes a 'miraculous' transformation into a BEAUTIFUL Butterfly, with brightly colored wings, so it is with the transformation of your potentials.

You may not look like what your potentials indicate today. That's because you are still in stage 2! That superstar artiste, world renown writer, fashion mogul, professional footballer is still in the Caterpillar stage. Wait for the process to be complete.

You may be mocked today. Well, you are in good company. They also mocked Albert Einstein, Walt Disney, Oprah Winfrey and many others too numerous to mention. Who would blame the mockers? After all, the Caterpillar LOOKS NOTHING LIKE THE BUTTERFLY.

From the larva stage, the development cycle of the butterfly moves to the pupa stage. Before the well-developed butterfly finally emerges into the light, scientists tell us that there is an intense struggle as the well-developed adult butterfly tries to 'break out'.

There is a popular story of a man who saw a butterfly struggling to come out of its cocoon and because of his love for butterflies; he couldn't stand to watch the 'poor creature' struggle for hours before breaking out. He tore the silky sack and out came the butterfly.

. You see, that 'struggle' was the much-needed strengthening process for exercising the butterfly's wing muscles and blood circulation. All the while the man thought he was helping the poor butterfly, he was actually hurting it by robbing it of the benefits of the struggling process.

The moral is that we should not be too hasty to leave our processing. It's a necessary part of the making of champions. The struggling process must be seen as an opportunity to develop character and you need strength of character to be truly effective in life. 'Ever heard the statement "Whatever doesn't kill you only makes you stronger?". That's the spirit.

The processing phase can be very uncomfortable. Stays focused and 'water' your potentials during this time as the process is a necessary part of your preparation for effectiveness. The process prepares you. The process purifies you by cutting off your pride and impatience. You've got to fall in love with the process of BECOMING.

Moses, a prominent bible character, had to go through a forty-year training process before he was ready to be one of the greatest leaders in history. Arrogance, gift-projection and impulsiveness are dealt with during the process. During the process, you learn discipline, resource management, humility and other similar virtues. In short, character building is a major hallmark of the process for those who allow the process to refine them. Have you seen anyone who did not go through a process? Like a half-cooked meal leaves a sour taste, such a person will not be effective.

Learn from David

Apart from learning, deliberate practice and undergoing mentorship, another critical action step during the process is packaging. Let me explain what I mean by packaging. As you develop your potentials into skills, begin to identify people who have problems that can be solved with your skills. Package a solution around your skills and offer it to them. Remember, people don't pay for potentials; they only pay for value. Your potential is linked to a problem. Find the problems closest to you that can be solved using your abilities and skills. I would like to illustrate this point with yet another interesting bible story (by now you may have guessed that I am a fan of bible stories).

Once upon a time[3], the Army of Israel had a problem. Their problem was a person; the person was their problem. His name was Goliath. He was a giant in the army of their sworn enemies - the Philistines, who were at this time in an open confrontation with the Israeli army. Goliath stepped forward and proposed a challenge for a head-to-head combat. He dared any Israeli soldier to come fight him saying that whoever won signified a win for the whole army. Everyone was afraid to fight this terrifying figure. Nobody dared volunteer; certainly not King Saul.

Personal Effectiveness

Before this time, young David the shepherd boy had developed his fighting potentials. He had become a skillful fighter by learning how to kill carnivorous animals seeking to devour his sheep. He came on the scene and learnt about the challenge. He simply offered his services and used his abilities to solve the problem at hand. He killed the giant and was rewarded with recognition and honor. The women composed a song for him and sang his praise in the streets. He became a National hero. In fact, he later became the King of Israel.

If your skills solve local problems, you become a local hero; if your skills solve national problems like David, you become a National hero. If your skills solve global problems, you become a global hero like Mark Zuckerberg, owner of *Facebook*.

Once when Saul, King of Israel had a problem (he suffered from what I may term acute depression) guess who had the most potent anti-depressant in all the realms? Yeah, you guessed right. David. His music was the anti-depressant that always saved the day. Any time the King was in a bad mood, David would play his instrument skillfully and the King would become fine. David was not only a skillful fighter but also a skillful instrumentalist and composer. Remember, he composed a lot of the songs in what we call the book of psalms in the bible.

Just like David your goal, therefore, is to package your potentials into problem-solving skills, identify the folks who have a problem you can solve, and then offer your solutions to them. For example, if you like to teach and you have

Process

teaching abilities, look for people who want to learn something you know which they don't. Offer to teach them. Trust me they won't refuse your offer.

Okay, it's a wrap for this chapter, but not without a few action steps.

Critical Action Steps

1) *Understand that all success is a process. Don't be in haste. Don't be grumpy or have a sour attitude. Work on your attitude.*
2) *The process is a time for training and learning. Build yourself. Read books . . . lots of books, at least one each month. Attend seminars and workshops, particularly in your area of interest and potentials.*

3) *Practice! Practice!! Practice!!! Turn your gifts into skills. Remember the 10,000 - Hour Rule.*
4) *Package a solution around your skills and offer it as a product or service. Look around your environment and find problems you are gifted and skilled at solving. In other words, think of a business you can build around your skill-set and start it.*

Chapter Three

Platform

There is yet another Bible story I must share. It is the story of a man who heard about Jesus and wanted to see Him. The only problem was that the crowd made it difficult to achieve his aim because he was of little stature. However he found a simple solution to his problem—he climbed a tree! Smart guy, don't you think? His strategy worked. Jesus not only saw him but offered to be his guest. Zacchaeus was his name. His story is a perfect analogy that explains the importance of what I am about to share: the power of platforms in your quest for personal effectiveness and success.

Personal Effectiveness

Where you stand matters because it determines who you see and who sees you. No matter how talented and skilled you are, if you're not being seen, no one thinks about you let alone patronize you. Be visible. Zacchaeus had to be seen by Jesus before any form of interaction could happen. If you are not seen, heard or noticed, no one will know and appreciate what you have to offer, let alone patronize you; and when you have no patronage, you get no profits just like the man in our opening story who buried his talent. If you recall, his master was very angry with him.

To be visible therefore, you need a platform. When you stand on a platform, you become very conspicuous. This is a true saying and applies both literally and figuratively speaking. That's why speakers, actors, and performers stand on platforms to deliver their content. Can you imagine addressing a crowd without a platform to stand? That would be horrible! You would not be able to grab the attention of your audience as many will struggle to see who is talking or performing and may consequently lose interest in what you have to say. There is something strategic and catchy about a platform.

Contextually, a platform can be defined as any opportunity to showcase what you've got to the right audience. It is a medium for announcing your skills.

Platform

 Lessons from Frank Edwards

Frank Edwards is a Nigerian gospel singer and producer. His first album, The Definition sold 100,000 copies on the first night it was released. If you've ever tried to promote a music CD, you'll understand that for an upcoming artiste back then and in these climes, selling that many copies in a single night was quite an achieve-ment. How did he perform such feat? Well, the album was produced by Love World Records, a music company owned by his local church and released at their gathering, the Night of Bliss program. What a good platform to be on. You must understand that first to have your album produced by such a brand (Love World Records) is first a platform. Then launching the album at a program which attracts hundreds of thousands of worshippers (like-minded folks) was another platform strategy. Phew!! It doesn't get any better than that.

You see, my friends, we must learn from Frank Edwards. His potential found a good platform to shine. Here's the lesson: Learn how to recognize and position yourself correctly on the right platforms.

You might be the most gifted person around, but

unless the right people see you and appreciate your value, you may never achieve maximum effectiveness and success in your life and career. For instance, it is arguable that one of the reasons why the Nigerian football maestro Austin Jay Jay Okocha did not get as many accolades, medals and trophies in his football career as other equally gifted footballers was because he never got into the right football clubs during his professional career. Most times even less gifted footballers win trophies when they play in the 'big clubs'. My point in all this is that **where you are matters as much as whom you are.**

 Show Thyself

Many years ago as members of the Nigerian youth Corp, I recall this slang popular amongst my circle of friends—and it went something like this: "show thyself ". Of course, it was the old English version of "Show yourself ". By this, we meant that one should display his or her (hopefully good) qualities for all to see. Generally speaking, in my country's vernacular, when one says 'You dey show yourself ', it is usually a disapproving way of telling you that you are trying too hard to get noticed. The point remains the same though. You need to put in the effort to be noticed.

A simple formula for sales and marketing is to put your products where your customers can see them. It is the same in selling your potentials: go where the prospects are.

In reality, dear friend as I think of all the movers and shakers I have both known and read about; and as I examine the successes I have achieved in my own life so far, I cannot deny the importance and efficacy of this strategy of 'showing yourself '. Sadly, I have seen mediocre performers rise to fame and fortune because of proper use of platforms while those with depth and quality have remained largely unknown and unsung as a result of their ignorance of the proper use of platforms.

How to Recognize and Maximize Platforms

Let's go over the major points so far.

1. Carefully identify your gifts and talents.
2. Develop your talents through a process of rigorous training and practice (hopefully under the watchful eye and guidance of a mentor).
3. Package a product and/or service around that gift that solves specific problems.

If you have followed me this far, now it is time to learn how to look for and seize great platforms.

Renowned American author and motivational speaker, Jim Rohn, was once invited to speak at his local Rotary Club function. Obviously, he did a good job of it because others began asking him to speak at their events. His training and speaking tours soon spread to several Rotary Club chapter engagements and other programs all over the world spanning over a period of forty years, until his demise in 2009. With the benefit of hindsight, one could say that his first opportunity to speak at that Rotary Club function was a platform. He made good use of his platform. Again, an opportunity to serve or solve a problem can be a platform to announce yourself to your world. Find your opportunity.

The man, Joseph

If you are familiar with the bible, then you should know about Joseph one of the sons of Jacob, popularly called *the dreamer*. Sold into slavery in a foreign land, he made his mark and rose to the post of Prime Minister in Egypt. How did he manage to rise from domestic slave to a top government official? His story reveals how to properly use a platform.

Joseph's platform began with an opportunity to solve a problem. The king had a dream he could not understand and needed an interpreter. Joseph, who had

Platform

the ability to interpret dreams (Potential) and had developed this gift through series of practice (remember he was interpreting the dreams of fellow inmates while in prison) was finally face to face with the most powerful man in the realm. That was a platform to showcase his skills. I'm sure you know the rest of the story.

Your platform may be a difficult problem you are called upon to solve.

As an employee, your current job may be a good platform in disguise. While you may not like the job very much but within your daily routine might just be the hidden opportunities you need for great profit in the future. Be wise.

Organizations, clubs and societies are good platforms to meet potential clients and position your unique offerings. A young man with great football skills for instance, should join a good football club where his skills can be noticed. Many notable footballers were first spotted while playing in local clubs.

Attend Seminars or Conferences that bring together people who love the kinds of things you do. See these meetings as platforms to introduce yourself and showcase your unique offering because, you are more likely to meet people who would value your skills and will be willing to pay for your offerings. Connect with people in your line of interest.

Relationships can also be platforms. Many have won contracts because of whom they know and who knows them. A dear friend of mine with whom I share fond memories of exploits during our campus days is currently a systems and strategy consultant with high profile clientele across different strata of society. He tells me that he works on projects even at the Federal Government level. I asked him how all these came to be. He said that a notable Professor in this country with strong business and political connections gave him his first 'shot' at consulting at that level even though he was yet unsure of himself. That was a platform; an opportunity.

Sometimes you need someone who believes in your potentials and skills, to mention you to the king. Form strategic alliances. Leverage on relationship platforms. Someone once said to an upcoming music star that "the key to success is to get discovered by a big shot".

How do you position yourself to be discovered by the big shots in your industry? It is by the proper use of platform. Today, in this 21st century the internet is one of the best platforms. No one has an excuse for lack of a platform to showcase their solutions since the World Wide Web if properly utilized, actually showcases your skills, gifts, and abilities to the whole world. Whatever products and services you have packaged using your skills and abilities can be properly showcased using the internet.

Platform

For instance, there is the option of setting up a blog where you regularly post your latest offerings; having a *Facebook* page or account; then there's *Whatsapp, Instagram,* and *Twitter.* There is also *YouTube* for uploading video contents. You can even have podcasts or send Newsletters. You can schedule an e-course to teach what you know to a willing audience. There are no limits to the methods and ways through which you can gain visibility using the internet. You can choose what medium suits you best. Choose your platforms carefully.

Victor, a friend of mine, tells me he just got scheduled to preach in Jamaica in a few weeks time. The invitation comes all expense paid. This would be his first international trip. I ask how he came about such a wonderful opportunity. His reply reaffirmed my belief in the power of the internet. He had been writing some thought-provoking and seemingly controversial articles on his Facebook wall. While some criticized him and argued with his content, an elderly lady from Jamaica was enjoying his depth of knowledge and began to follow him closely. At a point, she just felt that it was necessary to invite this young man to preach in her church. Please, this does not mean that everyone who writes great posts on social media would get international invitations. It is only a case in point to buttress the importance of utilizing the internet as a platform to showcase your brand.

Personal Effectiveness

I'm sure you can relate to this story somehow as there may be people you may know who have even gotten marriage proposals and other goodies through the same medium. Sadly, I know and have met some really gifted people whom I later searched for on the internet but could not find them. What a waste of the opportunity to be visible.

 See the Big Picture

Never despise a platform because it does not seem to be yielding cash just yet. Have you ever heard the term "From Free to fee"? Typically, you need platforms to showcase your worth for free at first. Many of the superstars today in the entertainment industry once had to do free shows and gigs before anyone was willing to pay them for anything. I dare say many of them almost begged to showcase their talents for free. Today, these same people charge in the millions to honour an invitation. That's how life works.

Take the comedy scene in Nigeria as a case study. For many big names today, Opa William's Night of a thousand laughs which began in 1995 was their platform. To be auditioned and given a slot (even for a few minutes) at such a platform was a major career boost. Many smart and talented comedians latched onto what seemed then to be the only available platform and became successful. Thankfully today there are many more of such platforms.

To be effective in the long run, you must be willing to take advantage of strategic platforms (by strategic platforms, I mean platforms that may not seem to yield profits now but may open bigger opportunities in the future). In a sense, I am teaching you to be futuristic in your thinking. See the big picture. Don't be stuck in the "here and now". All personally effective people see the big picture.

What are the take-home points we can begin to work on immediately? Here are some:

 Critical Action Steps

1) ***Google*** *your name or the name of your brand and see what comes up. If you don't like what you see, then it means there's work to be done.*
2) *Be visible. Even the man lame from his mother's womb was daily placed at the gate of the temple where people could see him (Acts 3:2). Seek out suitable platforms. Put your packaged solutions where people can see them and patronize you. You may need to sign up for a talent hunt, a reality show or any other similar platform in line with your gift. Remember that Ebuka Obi-Uchendu (popularly known as*

Personal Effectiveness

Ebuka), became a household name after appearing at the 'Big Brother Nigeria' reality show in 2006 even though he didn't win. For Frank Edwards, it was his Church program. Jim Rohn had Rotary Club to thank for his own opportunity. Someone reading this may have to join a writers' club or a speakers' club to get their first opportunity. Attend seminars, join clubs, and make friends with great minds. Connect strategically.

3) *Be active on social media. Today, thanks to the internet, no one has an excuse for not being visible. Open a **Facebook** account or page for your brand. And then there's **Whatsapp, Twitter** and **Instagram**. For example, fashion experts use blogs and tools like **Instagram** to promote their unique offers. The same can be done for any other sphere. Social media is not for silly jokes and nude pictures! It's a platform for marketing your value. Use it wisely.*

4) *If you are currently employed, see your job as a platform to display your skills and ability. Be your best always. You never know who is watching and where your next recommendation will come from. I also strongly encourage all working class professionals to have an active **LinkedIn** account. It is one of the most suitable platforms for career professionals in the 21st century. There are many people who have been discovered by suitable employers through it.*

Platform

In summary, prepare for platforms and pursue platforms.

Chapter Four

Profit

'Profit' referred to in this context includes all the benefits available for correctly discovering, developing and deploying your unique skills and abilities. They include monetary gains (riches), fulfillment and recognition. These are the rewards for solving problems with your potentials (talents and skills).

The man, who endeavors to do his best with all the resources available to him, will not only acquire money as a reward for solving problems; he would also be satisfied

Profit

knowing that his life is making a difference in the world. Recognition and honor will also be due him even after his death.

A quick advice about pricing is important at this juncture. Although product pricing is a subject of its own and I do not intend to cover that in this book, suffice to say that you should never be afraid to put a good price on what you have to offer. Don't sell yourself cheap. Know when to do free stuff and when to ask for a fee. The plan is to profit from your potentials and you can't get full profit doing "free shows" all the time.

Sometimes the profit will be in the form of promotion at your place of work. You may become the head of the establishment like David and Joseph became King and Prime Minister respectively. Other times, profit will come with great recognition and fame particularly if your gift lies around sports and entertain-ment. Remember, the women composed songs for David after he killed Goliath. He became famous.

There's a song by a Nigerian Artiste who goes by the stage name Praiz titled "Rich and Famous". The lyrics capture the kind of things that happen when your harvest time has come. Not only will you have money in abundance, you will also become famous in your own way. Now being famous here is clearly a subjective language. But I'm sure you get the gist.

For me, by far the best profit is having that sense of

Personal Effectiveness

fulfillment, an inner sense of accomplishment and satisfaction knowing that I am daily becoming the best version of myself and solving the problems I was uniquely designed to solve; and that when all is said and done, I can look back and say I 'made a dent in the universe' as Steve Jobs would say.

 Critical Action Steps

---

1) *If you are not profiting from your talents it may be because you are not adequately marketing and selling your unique solutions. Sell yourself more.*

2) *If you require more platforms to be visible then, by all means, go for more.*

3) *Stop selling yourself cheap. Know when to give free and know when to ask for a fee. Put a price on your skills.*

Closing

According to Norman Cousins, "Death isn't the greatest loss in life. The greatest loss is what dies inside us while we live".

In summary, to profit through your potentials, you must first take stock of your unique gifts and skill sets. Thereafter, you are to prepare and package these unique gifts into a unique solution usually through a process requiring plenty practice. Your unique solution can either be a product (a book, a musical album, a well-designed outfit) or a service (babysitting, teaching, auto repairs).

You are then required to position and promote your prepared and packaged products and services on suitable platforms so that those in need of them can readily locate you. This you can do mostly by attending the right functions and joining the right organizations as well as being active on social media (amongst other things).

Personal Effectiveness

When these P's (**potentials** packaged through a **process** and positioned on a **platform**) are taken care of, then the final P (which is **profit**) must come. It is an unfailing formula for productivity and personal effectiveness.

I hope with these few words of mine . . . (laughs), Okay, maybe not so few words after all. All the same, as I end this little book, I hope you get the gist that a truly effective life is one which fulfills its twin purpose of productivity and profit.

May you have the wisdom to know what to do (with your gifts and talents), the courage to do what you know and the persistence to keep 'doing' until your profit comes.

I believe in your potentials.

Endnotes

1. M.M.M. stands for Mavrodi Mundial Movement. Considered by many as a ponzi scheme company with subsidiaries in 118 countries, its participants, however, maintain that it is a Global fund of mutual aid as monies are contributed in a community through benevolent acts of giving and receiving with percentage interest.

2. A slang used in Nigeria loosely translated as; 'Who has Potential helped? Or, 'Of what benefit is Potential?'

3. The story of David and Goliath can be read in the Bible in the book of First Kings Chapters 17.

Personal Effectiveness

www.ingramcontent.com/pod-product-compliance
Lightning Source LLC
Chambersburg PA
CBHW030036230526
45472CB00002B/543